Dear, you?

Geddin Bautista

BookLeaf Publishing

India | USA | UK

Presentation by *BookLeaf Publishing*

Web: www.bookleafpub.com

E-mail: info@bookleafpub.com

ISBN: 9789358315196

First edition 2023

To my parents, and my best friend.

ACKNOWLEDGEMENT

I don't blame anyone for the lack of merriment in my writing, but I thank the ones I love for understanding my constant cries. Although I may not be the most honest-hearted, I appreciate the people who let me be true. For my best friend, for who I'll stay always by your side, the one who saves me from becoming a dove. And for my mother who is my light, the roots my stem needed to shoot. The two people I love the most, thank you.

PREFACE

My writing comes from the thoughts hidden behind the doors in my mind, too afraid to open my mouth and hear others' reactions. These thoughts may come from personal experiences, or what I have heard from other people. Hence, I write from multiple points of view, to allow everyone to empathize, to allow everyone to relate; to allow everyone to think and feel the words being said, and the questions being asked.

Aurora

She was rain;
Seraphic in disguise.
Like these falling drops of silver,
She washed away the tears which slithered from
my eyes.
As she cried and thundered,
I didn't shield myself from her storms,
But stood and embraced her,
As the water pierced through my skin to my
bones.
The peace brought by the pattering was
pacifying.
Her gentle whispers voyaged through my ears.
Until each constellation glistened,
Until her voice was all I could hear.

To be a dove

Look at me like the prettiest sunset.
Look at me the way they see the moon.
No matter her shape,
She's still the beauty of the dark blue.
Why is it so hard to be seen,
Why is it so hard to be loved,
As a human in this distorted world;
To think the only solution is to jump.
The only way to bloom,
To be as beautiful as a dove.
'Til I rise and become a star,
Is that when you'll finally acknowledge?
Is that when you'll finally see?
Am I finally worth your attention,
As my cold body comes into the scene?

What is worth?

Afraid to admit.
Ashamed to be alive.
Why must I bear the cuts she leaves on my skin?
Why must I keep the bruises he leaves on my
body?
All so he could be raised to be "manly enough,"
All so she could be raised to be "beautiful
enough,"
To discover it really meant to be "good enough."
But what does it really mean to be

"Enough?"

What is worth if not one being can fit in its
shoes?

Where should I look for you?

I wondered why we distanced ourselves.
I wondered why we loved each other,
If we were only meant to choose,
None other than to move apart when the flames
grew bigger.

Why not speak?
Why not urge?
Why not break through the bars that kept us
apart?
Why conceal if we vowed to be true?

If humans were like sentences,
If we were the words,
I wondered why we couldn't break the distance
between each other.
I wondered why we would only make sense if
there were voids between us.
I wondered if those letters also longed to fill the
gaps.

To be a man who can express,
To be a woman who can understand,
Why aren't you here?
Why must I beg to be by your side?

Maybe in another life.

Do you think of me when you see him?
Do you think of the footsteps you left on my
chest?
Does a fragment of your mind,
Remember an ounce of my existence?

Can you hear my screams when you pick up a
lighter?
Can you see the tears fall when you bring it
closer to your lips?
Does a fragment of your mind,
Remember an ounce of my pleads?

What's his favourite food?
What's his favourite colour?
Does a fragment of your mind,
Remember what mine were?

I hope you give him back the time I should have
had.
I hope you lift him in your arms how you used to
with me.
Because my entire mind,
Remembers what used to be mine.

How strong you are

I envied the smoke which left your mouth,
Seeming as though it was needed more than I
was.
Despite putting my lungs in chains,
You still sought it more than you did me.
Your absence stole my trust;
Yet your empty promises continued.
But the woman you had me with taught me,
How to win against a rock with paper;
How to win against a bullet with glass;
How to be proud of the lady I've become.
As she was the roots my stem needed to shoot.
As she was the sun and rain I needed to grow.
You gave me the answer to all my whys.
You left me with a gift worth more than the
stars.
Yet I still hold love for both my blood,
But for her I would protect with my life…

Set you free

Would you understand me if I told you,
I couldn't see a difference from the first time,
The first time that you held me,
To the last time you saw me cry?

Why am I the same person?
The same knot in your mind you can't undo.
You think of me as a treasure,
But must I make your life so blue?

What can I do to make it better?
How can I free you from their shackles?
How do I treat the scars their words cut?
How can I sharpen the blades you use in your battles?

What is the price of happiness?
Why must the cost be your pain?
I'm trying to change to see you smile,
I'm trying to change so they no longer reign.

Too late

A flower whose petals were picked too soon.
To blossom too early was inevitably her fate.
She sat at the bridge between the world and all
that was after.
As a clock whose palms touched too late.
How had he not seen how they tormented her?
How had he not seen the red in her eyes?
How her face no longer glowed,
How her skin trembled at their lies.
How her lips were now a pool,
Where her tears swum onto her tongue;
And a mouthful of heartache,
Became a mouthful of smoke down her lungs.

Purple or red?

Unable to recognize,
The unfamiliar face,
Whose eyes held a young girl.
Encapsulated by her own fate.
Her own vines wrapped 'round her body.
Trapped as the thorns grip onto her skin.
Fighting against her own plots.
To avenge the anger shes bottled within.
Now that purple must battle red,
Which side did she want to win?
Was she to stay afraid until the end?
Or use her fire to blaze her last sins?

His

Let me feel your touch,
Your fingers trace my lips.
Your hands cup my cheeks,
Then move down to my hips.
Let me see your smile,
How do I fall each time?
Your dimples I admire,
The times I stare should be a crime.
Let me be the shoulder for your tears,
Embrace you when they scream.
Hold you when their lightning reaches,
When they strike your chest so clean.
Why are you afraid to take it off?
Take off the mask when you're with me.
Why conceal if we're in love?
Or is it harder than it seems?

The one who figured it out

To be raised in a town of trees,
Trees that never learned how to flower.
How could she not have gotten lost?
How could she ever get back those hours?
Walking along the ground's veins,
Walking along its widening lips,
Not one person in that town,
Didn't have a heart full of rips.
Like a snake her bark shed,
Her branches twisted and brewed flames.
And that's how she,
Brought wolfsbane to her name;
Ethereally deadly to touch.
As each of her petals were blades.
As each of her buds were arrows.
Shot by the hands which were ablaze.

Life

I watch the raindrops race down the glass,
I watch as the water falls to my lap.
Her screams silenced by the explosions;
Her tears rise up as they turn black.
And her smile ripped away by betrayal.
Neglect was her will to survive.
To survive in her dystopia.
Scattering through the sea of what was once her
home.
She was a ship in battle.
Sweating bullets into their throne.
As waves raged onto her skin.
Gnawing its teeth into her veins,
And gliding its tongue at all he found red.
Thus her blood continued to beg.

But one pondering question,
Remained to sit quietly in her mind.
Floating in a pool of resentment.
Why? Why? Why?

How could they make a child,
A pawn in their heinous game?
But one leap of perseverance,
Could make the whole world know her name.

She'll never learn

Please pick up the phone.
I don't know where you have been.
If you aren't inside my head,
Does this mean you can't be seen?
Does this mean I've moved on?
Moved on from that face,
Moved on from those eyes,
Moved on from the delusions,
Did God hear my cries?
Does my life finally belong,
Is it no longer in your control,
Does it now belong to me?
Or have I gotten it all wrong?
Why do I hear another?
Another one to bow down to.
Another pair of hands,
Wrapped 'round my waist way too soon.
To trap what beats inside my chest.
To trap the girl whose mouth stays taped.
Silenced by each finger they press against her,
Afraid to protest against her fate.

A losing game

A flower trying to blossom in winter;
He was a seed seeking sunlight and water.
His petals fragile in the cold,
From the bitterness of the surrounding weather.
Hence our skin grazed to detain warmth,
His cheeks blush from our touch.
But when we parted ways he would lose it all.
Concealing himself behind the snowmen.
Covering himself in icicles.
Masking himself with a plastered smile.
And I watched him fade once the rain stopped.
As he sharpened his thorns,
In case someone were to invade the peace.

Dear my love,

15

How much longer can we stay?
How much longer will you refuse,
Refuse to admit how it's too true;
Refuse to ignite the fuse.
Why do you say we are forever?
Why do you promise to always be,
To always help me remember,
That only I'm allowed to see,
To see the little boy behind that smile,
And see the child who no one loved.
So let me be the girl who does;
Who saves you from above.

Don't need you anymore

Can't you need me the way a fire needs to burn?
Can't you need me the way a car needs fuel?
Can't you need me the way books need to be
read?
Can't you want me the way that I do you?

What does she have that I don't?
What does she give you that I can't?
What is hers that isn't mine?
Why must I share my name with her blood?

I see her swap her thorns for your seeds.
I see her plant them into ur bed.
I watch as your children blossom,
I watched them grow as my arms bled.

Nothing is forever

How did we become,
These mere squares in a screen?
Why did our words turn into muffles?
Why do their hands hold our screams?

Have you ever wondered what it feels like,
To be stuck behind the glass?
Behind those bars forever,
What's the point if we can't last?

Why must these pictures be taken?
Why must these memories be kept?
If one cannot remember,
What's its worth if not to be left?

Let me stay

I think it's okay to want to stay.
I think it's okay to not want to grow.
Until I have met a person,
Who's ripped more than they can sew.
Until I have met that person,
Who's swam further than they could row.
Only then I won't ask
"Why can't I stay as her little girl?"
But how can I truly want to live,
If she's already given me the world?

For you I will stay

That day I figured it out;
That there was no way for me to leave.
Even as I recalled the words you said to her,
Even as I came to realize,
That this whole time you weren't mine.

I learned what it meant to be in love,
I learned to seek the truth behind the eyes,
As tears streamed down your face,
As they washed away your lies.

When you came and sought my arms,
And I gently wrapped them 'round your neck,
Did you know how badly,
You had turned me to a wreck?

Did you know how much I hurt?
Could you see the wrenching pain beneath my
skin?
Could you see the resentment that I buried,
Buried deep so you could win?

I couldn't listen to you any further,
You knew how much I hated hearing you say,
How much I hated you talk about yourself,

In your dehumanizing ways.

I was the one that needed comfort,
I was the one that should've been held.
So tell me if it was fair,
To feel guilty for all I said.

I kept the knife you stabbed inside me,
I kept the stains you left on my clothes,
As a way to always honor,
This day that no one knows.

The art of solitude

Do you know what really scares me?
To survive alone in a storm.
Because what's the point of living,
If I live to be alone?
Why should I fight to stay afloat,
On top of a mere piece of wood?
Why shouldn't I let the water take me,
Even if I know that it could?
But why do we think of it this way?
Why do we think that we'd be doomed?
If the world began with just a seed,
Can't one try to lift the mood?
To turn fate upside down,
To turn it all the way around,
Perhaps to be one without a partner,
Will be the most beautiful sound.

Push out of love

I stared at the walls that you used to,
I saw the words your eyes left.
Like using blood to paint the letters,
Like carving your pleads onto stone,
Your eyes engraved a message,
Telling me not to leave you alone.

This is what she would do for you,
Would you have ever done the same?
No, you stabbed her with the ice in your hands,
Watching her eyes close without shame.

How could anyone ever love you?
If you keep pushing them away,
If you freeze them out so cold,
How could they find a way to stay?